Dedicated to Addie and Alisa with love.

HAPPY EASTER
This book belongs to:

BUNNY

KISSES!

EASTER
WISHES!

HIPPITY

HOPPITY!

HAPPY
EASTER

Happy Easter!

HAPPY

EASTER!

HAPPY

SPRING!

WELCOME

SPRING!

HAPPY

SPRING!

HAPPY
EASTER!

EASTER

BLESSINGS

Made in the USA
Monee, IL
18 March 2023

30163761R00057